The A - Z
of EBook Publishing

An Easy Step-by-step guide to go from
NO IDEA to Massive EBook PROFITS

EDIRIN EDEWOR
Foreword by Steve Harris

DEDICATION

This book is dedicated to everyone who has a book inside of them. Your book is a gift; share it with the world already.

FOREWORD

I've always thought Edirin Edewor to be shy and introspective. Big mistake. That's why nothing could have prepared me for the masterpiece that is "The A - Z of Ebook Publishing". While I've been privileged to be a small part of this amazing undertaking, I truly can't take the credit.

Edirin, an authority in her own right, was humble enough to take my advice, to write about something that the thought leadership market was hungry and willing to pay for; becoming an internationally renowned best selling author. As an author with some modest success, I've dreamed of seeing these words after my bio... "New York Times Best Selling Author" or "Amazon Best Selling Author".

Now, while I've always imagined the "when", I've always been clueless about the "how". Not anymore. With Edirin Edewor's easy to follow "how to" masterpiece, this is the go to book for any established or emerging author to follow to get your hopefully, really good book on the best seller's list.

Thanks Edirin. I can't wait to execute on this! It's no longer a matter of "when", because thanks to you, I know "how"

Steve Harris

Life & Business Strategist &

(Soon to be Internationally Acclaimed Best Selling) Author

ACKNOWLEDGEMENTS

First of all, I acknowledge God in whom I move, breathe and have my being. All I am today is because of Him. I am forever grateful. I appreciate my mum Edna Edewor for being my number 1 fan, for not telling me to go get a job and be normal, and for being patient with me while I was trying to find myself.

To my mentor John Obidi for being the absolute best, for straightening me up when I gave excuses, for believing in me even when I didn't believe in myself and for being an amazing friend. To my awesome Coach Steve Harris for living up to his title as Ruthless Executioner and for holding me accountable till I finished writing this book with time to spare, for coaching me with wisdom, understanding and firmness.

To my friends Remi Owadokun, Bode Agbe-Davies, Nnanke Essien and Iguehi Aletor for being patient and understanding when I would whine about the book not being enough or being too much. Last but not the least, to Tami-Jade De la Guerre for always checking up on me and encouraging me, even though we've never met and live in different countries. I never forget good people. Thank you.

LEGAL DISCLAIMER

This book and the content provided therein are simply for educational purposes and to serve as a guide to writing, publishing, marketing and profiting from eBooks. All information contained in this book are deemed accurate as at the time of publishing. However, this is not an exhaustive treatment of the subjects and expert opinions may differ.

Any use of this information is at your own risk. the author does not assume and hereby disclaims any liability to any party or any loss, damage or disruptions caused by errors or omissions resulting from accident, negligence or any other cause.

No guarantees of income or profits are intended by this book. Many variables affect each individual's results. Your results will vary from the results given. The author does not accept responsibility for your results. If you wish to apply ideas contained in this book, you are taking full responsibility for your choices, actions and results.

Copyright © 2017 Edirin Edewor.

All rights reserved. No part of this publication may be reproduced, distributed, or transmitted in any form or by any means, including photocopying, recording, or other electronic or mechanical methods, without the prior written permission of the publisher, except in the case of brief quotations embodied in reviews and certain other non-commercial uses permitted by copyright law.

TABLE OF CONTENTS

Dedication	2
Foreword	3
Acknowledgments	4
Legal Disclaimer	5
Table of Contents	6
Introduction	7
Chapter one: Book Writing Myths	13
Chapter two: Coming Up with an Idea for Your Book	19
Chapter three: The Process of Writing Your Book	24
Chapter four: Editing, Subtitles and Book Cover Design	32
Chapter five: Publishing on Amazon	38
Chapter six: The Launch	42
Chapter seven: Marketing Your Book Effectively	49
Chapter eight: Repurposing Your eBook Content for More Profit	58
Conclusion	63
About the Author	64
Connect with Me	65

INTRODUCTION

WHY YOU SHOULD BE WRITING AN E-BOOK

Let me start by saying congratulations to you! The fact that you got this book means you believe you have a book inside of you and you want to get it out. That's more than a lot of people have ever done. Did you know that 70% of Americans wish they could write a book but less than 1% of them ever make an effort to begin? The reasons for this are very many and quite legitimate.

Many people want to write and publish a book but they don't know where to start from. Traditional publishing firms are very selective in who they publish books for. Most times, they will only publish books of people who already have some form of success in their field and are well-known. You have to be pretty great at something or be a really good writer before they will grant you audience. Too many manuscripts lie in dust in the offices of publishing houses, delaying and even shattering the dreams of many a writer.

Some other people do not believe they have what it takes to write something that people will actually read - wether it's fiction or non-fiction. They are unsure of their abilities to write something that will captivate an audience. For some people still, they know how to write but have no publishing agencies or their own money to print books and market them to become profitable. Let's face it. It is easier for publishers to print and market your book for you than it is to do it out of your own pocket. I mean, what are the guarantees that you will be able to sell all your books, recover your investment and make profit off of it? It's too risky.

This is just one of the fears that self published authors have to deal with. They also have to do the promotions, marketing, advertisement and sales by themselves or shell out huge sums of money to advertising agencies with no guarantees of success. They end up spending thousands of dollars and yet, less than 50% of the time does the book actually do well enough to cover the cost of publishing and promoting, barely making any profit. This is not a good system if you want to earn a decent income and achieve financial freedom from writing books.

The independent publishing industry or indie publishing industry for short, has seen a rise in recent years. More and more indie authors are writing and publishing amazing books and are making a killing out of it. Amazon kindle publishing has created a Billion dollar industry for authors and boasts of more independently published books than any other platform on earth. A lot of indie authors have been able to make six and seven figure income annually, both directly and indirectly from their books.

The rise in digital media has seen more and more people opt for digital versions of books which has prompted traditional publishers to publish electronic versions of their books, called eBooks. Amazon Kindle, iBooks, Nook and other online book stores are stocking more and more eBooks and the majority of these books are from self published authors like me.

The benefits of publishing an eBook far outweigh those of publishing print books. First of all, indie authors make more money from eBooks than print books. This is because of the huge growth market for eBooks. Also, there are no overhead costs. I literally spent $0 creating, publishing and marketing my first book on Amazon (mostly because I had no idea what I was doing at the time and I'm too thrifty to spend money doing what I had no idea of), but somehow, I was able to hack my way to #15 on the bestsellers list in my niche and #8,130 in the Kindle Store in less than a week! By the way, you have to be a rock star to be in the top 100 in your niche and the top 20,000 in the kindle store.

The best part is that there is no need for inventory and shipping costs. You don't have to worry about printing a thousand copies of your book and then nobody buys; or having to ship books all over the country or around the world. You also don't have to worry about your book copies running out. Your book, once published, is there forever in infinite copies and will make money for you forever as long as it keeps selling. There are authors who are still making money from a book they published 5 years ago. Now, that's what passive income is all about - you do the job once and it keeps paying over and over and over again.

The barrier of entry for eBook publishing is low. Literally anyone can publish a book. Of course, this presents a problem with quality as every Tom, Dick and Irene can write anything and publish it. It's now left for you and me to put out really good quality books that people will read and be grateful to us for writing. Low barrier of entry means you don't have to be an expert or a professor in a subject before you can write about it. You just have to know a little more than your reader audience to write something for them.

If you are writing a book about success, you don't have to be Bill Gates before you write that kind of book. There are people who just want to get to your level of success and will be grateful for a book that can show them how to achieve that. Someone who's dead broke may not have the capacity to handle the processes that the super-successful people talk about.

The benefits of publishing an eBook are immense. I published a simple 19-page eBook called The Productivity Checklist as a passion project/experiment with no guide or experience and it went up to #15 in my category and #8,130 in the kindle store within a week and has sold hundreds of copies even though I have stopped marketing it. Writing that book helped me come out of depression, find my purpose in life and launched a new career that has been nothing short of awesome.

Writing that book changed my life. I became an almost-instant celebrity, built authority in the thought leadership community in my country, created multiple streams of income directly and indirectly and I have been able to help other people write and publish their own books with stellar results. I want to help you do the same too, that's why I am writing this book. Maybe it will change your life like it did mine, maybe it will not; but I'm willing to bet that it will.

Now, I can't guarantee you that reading this book will make you tons of money and give you the results that I and my students have had. It doesn't work that way. However, I can tell you that if you make a decision to follow the easy step-by-step guide in this book, you will have no excuse for not getting your book published on Amazon. You will be better able to write your book in no time, with little or no cost, and make a decent profit. You will learn how to turn your one book into multiple streams of income that if done consistently, will create time and financial freedom for you.

My first book on Amazon, one week after publishing.

A WORD OF CAUTION:

Before you continue to the next chapter, you have to reach a resolution that you will write your book and publish it. If you have no intention of taking action, please keep this book till when you are ready. This book is for serious people only. But if you are tired of waiting, procrastinating and giving yourself bullshit (excuse my language) excuses as to why you haven't yet written your book, please keep reading.

This book is an action guide that is intended to help you hit the publish button before you are through reading it. It doesn't matter if it takes you three weeks or three months to complete this book, but by the end of the last chapter, you should have a potential bestseller on your bookshelf on Amazon. I wish you all the best!

CHAPTER ONE:

COMMON BOOK WRITING MYTHS

I have heard many Book writing myths from all kinds of people, even authors themselves. To me, these are all just bullshit excuses that keep people from writing. When I published my first book thankfully, I had no idea these myths existed. I just googled a lot, got a sketchy idea of how the publishing was done and then wrote and published my book in six days. I did everything myself. From finding the idea, putting together the content, writing, editing, publishing and promoting.

I did a few "trial and error" promotions on social media that ended up being the single biggest factor that helped my book reach #15 in my category and #8130 on the kindle store. Mind you, there are millions of books in the Kindle store and as I said earlier, if your book makes the top 20,000, you are a Rock star. All indie authors agree with this.

So what are these myths that may be keeping you from writing and publishing your e-book?

MYTH #1: **WRITING IS NOT FOR EVERYONE**

First of all, I call BS on that. Everyone has a book inside of them. You don't have to be a professor or a college graduate or even a GED Holder to write a book. I can go on to list books that have been written by people with no education that are New York Times bestsellers but I won't. A lot of people are stuck in this state. They feel that they have to be an expert at something before they write a book about it, but that's not true. How many dieting books are written by nutritionists? How many business books are written by people who own multi-million dollar businesses? How many food recipe books are written by professional chefs?

Hey, I wrote a book on Productivity but I wasn't a productivity expert. If you are very good at something, you can write a book about it. If you feel you don't know enough, Google is your friend. Get rid of the mindset blocks that are stopping you from writing your book. Your life is rich with experiences that you can draw from and gift the world with the awesomeness that is you.

MYTH #2: YOU HAVE TO BE AN AUTHORITY TO WRITE A BOOK

Ummm... you are an authority on the subject of YOU. You are an expert at being you. No one knows you better than you. No one knows what lessons you've learned from your experiences, your family, your job, your challenges, your failures and your successes. Did you fail in business? Write a book on how to fail in business. Are you a reformed ex convict? Write a book on your journey to redemption. Were you a college dropout turned success? Write a book on that (wait... I think there is already a book on that). Are you a struggling or thriving single mom? Share your struggles and triumphs. Are you really good at your job? Write an instruction guide on what it is that you do that makes you a superstar.

Being an authority is actually the other way round. You don't have to become an authority before you write a book. Writing makes you an authority. Want to become an authority in your field? Write a quality book about a subject in your field. I wasn't an authority on productivity, but writing a book on productivity made me an authority. Besides, a book is the new business card. Give out your card at networking events and you may be forgotten but give out a link to get your book? Instant celebrity!

MYTH #3: I DON'T LIKE WRITING SO I CANNOT WRITE A BOOK

So many people struggle with this. I didn't. I always loved writing, but so many other people struggle with this. Maybe you do too. Maybe you have tried writing before, but you find yourself staring at a blank screen for hours (I hope you haven't tossed your PC yet). That's okay. Not everyone has the super special talent of picking up a pen and having the words flow like a river (Believe it or not, I'm on a roll writing this here).

There are a lot of people like you who actually hate writing but have written several books. What if I told you that there is a super easy way to get your book out of your head and published without having to write it, a way so simple you would probably face-palm yourself when you found out? Keep reading, we will get there.

MYTH #4: NO ONE WILL BUY MY BOOK

Many indie authors struggle with this one. Traditional publishers will usually do all the PR, marketing and advertising so the author just sits back and let the checks roll in. With indie authors however, we tend to do it all by ourselves. Most times, authors get so overwhelmed with the promotions, marketing strategy, advertising and sales, that they put off writing the book altogether. They end up doing everything but the one thing they should be focused on, and that is writing.

It is a legitimate challenge, especially if you're a first-time author, or if you are unknown. However, remember that everyone starts off at ground zero, but with simple, inexpensive marketing strategies that I will be sharing with you in chapters 6 and 7, you will be on your way to an Amazon bestseller and bring in the money. Indie authors have a huge potential in eBook publishing and it is left to you to grab your share in this industry.

MYTH #5: I NEED TO WRITE MORE BOOKS IN ORDER TO SELL

I hear a lot of indie authors say this and I am baffled. The people who do this either do not have very good marketing strategies or do not have a life. No one can really rely on writing several high-quality books each year in order to make a decent profit. The right marketing systems can turn one book into several streams of income. One book can create passive income if done right, and I will be showing you how to do it right. You don't need to worry about writing several books a year if you want to earn a living writing.

Every kind of excuse can be grouped into one of these writing myths. Anyone can write a book. You don't have to be a genius or an authority before you write a book. Writing and publishing an e-book is practically inexpensive, and with the right systems you can milk your eBook for more money than you ever thought possible. Even If you have no idea on what to write, the next chapter will deal with that. It is at this point that I urge you to bring out your pen and notepad because it's about to get practical. Please follow the guides and apply them as you read along. This way, you should have your awesome book published by the end of this book.

CHAPTER TWO:

COMING UP WITH AN IDEA FOR YOUR BOOK

I mentioned earlier that a lot of people will like to write a book, but they have no idea what to write. If that is you, keep reading. When I decided I was going to write a book, I had no idea what to write about. I was dealing with a lot of personal things so I was unwilling to write about myself and my challenges. I wanted to be done with that phase of my life before writing anything about it.

Now, I had an interior design company and a bead-making company which I ran from home. I knew that learning time management and being productive were the keys to me getting my work done and hitting my goals, so I decided to write about that. I asked my family and a few friends what they thought about the idea and they loved it.

The purpose of my book was to challenge myself to do something I had never done before and to inspire people to go after their dreams too. It was a passion project. I have been able to achieve both of these things, so I will say I was successful with my book.

HOW TO FIND AN IDEA FOR YOUR BOOK

STEP 1: FIND THE PURPOSE OF YOUR BOOK

You need to first get clear on your WHY. Why do you want to write a book? What do you want to achieve by writing this book? This helps you get clarity on what you want so that you can get super focused. It makes the process easier. If you don't have a WHY, you won't get started, and even if you do, you won't finish.

This is one of the biggest reasons why some people get stuck on a book for years and never finish it. Is your purpose to make money? To build a reputation like a platform for a career in speaking, coaching and consulting? Do you want to be able to grow your network? or is it a passion project?

Your reason will determine the course you will take in the writing, the content and the marketing of your book. This helps to manage your expectations. If you are writing a passion project, you would not expect to make a ton of money because you are focusing on the impact rather than the income.

For first-time writers, I will advise you don't focus on the money solely. Focus on a deeper purpose so you can enjoy the journey of writing and publishing. This ensures you don't put yourself under undue pressure by comparing your earnings with authors who have experience, an audience and money to boost their sales.

STEP 2: WHAT IS YOUR BOOK GOING TO BE ABOUT?

The next step is to ask yourself what your book is going to be about. This step can be quite difficult, especially if you have no idea what you want to write about. There are four ways by which you can get ideas for your book:

1. Look within yourself. What do you know? What is the one thing you're good at? What do people ask you for help on the most? What advice do you give with ease? What part of your story inspires people? What hack have you discovered that works well for you that you can share with people? You may find out that you know more than you give yourself credit for.

2. Ask people what they think you could talk about with ease. When asking yourself doesn't seem to be yielding any results, ask your friends and family. Listen to them and find a recurring word or phrase. They may just know more about your abilities than you do.

3. Ask your audience. If you have an audience on social media, your blog or mailing list, ask them what problems they have that they think you can help them solve. You can also just straight up ask them for ideas on book topics you can write on. Chances are, if they think you can write a book on a subject, they would most likely buy it.

4. Research your niche on Amazon. After looking within

yourself and asking around and you come up with a recurring word or phrase, for example: fitness, lose weight, eat right, Sixpack abs etc, it should give you an idea of what category to write on. In you're into fitness, these phrases or words shouldn't come as a surprise. The next step is to do your research to narrow in on a subject by going on Amazon. Here's how you do this:

a) Go to Amazon to do some digging.

b) Go to Kindle books

c) Go to the Kindle bestsellers

d) Go to the category you are researching on (e.g Fitness)

e) Go to a subcategory similar to your keywords (e.g Nutrition)

f) Look at books that are the bestsellers there and look at the keywords. Keywords help you know how to come up with a topic in a profitable category.

g) You want to look at books within a reasonable price range (e.g. $0.99-4.99) as a first time author.

h) Take note of their ranking on Amazon's Kindle store (less than 20,000 is good), Ranking in their niche/category (less than 100 is good), Number of pages (less than 150 is good, remember you're a first time author), the book title, the description and reviews.

i) Find a popular keyword and choose that to write about (e.g. Paleo diet, gluten-free, vegan, keto diet).

j) Pick 1-3 books on this subject and research them. You want to write on the subject that is doing well, but add your own uniqueness to it.

k) Come up with a catchier title from your competition. Remember you want to stand out.

l) Alternatively, if you don't see a book similar to what you would like to write, it might be that there is a hole in the market and you can fill it. OR the reason no one is writing about it is because it isn't a good idea.

This process helps you get clarity for the next phase which is the writing process. Remember you have found the purpose for your book, you know what your book is going to be about and you have done your research on Amazon to validate the idea and come up with a catchy title. Now it is time to start writing. Let's get to it!

CHAPTER THREE:

THE PROCESS OF WRITING YOUR BOOK

Yes! You're finally here. You have come up with your book title and you have a pretty good idea of what you want to write about. Feels good, doesn't it? But you can just grab your pen and notepad or your PC and start writing away. This is one major mistake most people make. That is why they have writers' block and all the other writing related challenges. However, that is not going to happen to you because I am going to show you a simple three-step process that'll get your book out of your head and into Amazon Kindle (or your website or wherever you wanna put it).

The truth is, even after refining and validating your idea, it can still be vague. I have written books, I have taught webinars and online courses on how to publish an e-Book but when it came to writing this book, I didn't just jump on it even though I can teach e-Book publishing in my sleep. I had to go through these three steps too, and as that when I started to actually write, I wrote the introduction and the first two chapters in less than a day. At the end of this book I will say how long it took me to write it. My accountability buddy is wrote the foreword for this book and he will be corroborating it too.

This three-step process is really simple and it helps you gain more clarity on what the book will be about and eliminate the issue of writers' block, blank PC screens and broken laptops. Here it is:

MIND MAP ⟶ OUTLINE ⟶ WRITE

Did I hear you say, "is that it?" Yes it is. It's that simple. Once you follow this three-step process, I guarantee you that you will get your book done in no time. No more blank pages. No more screaming at nothing. No more broken things. Just the sweet sight of your already finished book. It is not only effective in writing your whole book, but also in the chapter by chapter writing of your book. This process will help you get your book written fast, one chapter at a time. So what are these steps exactly?

STEP 1: MIND MAP

Mind mapping involves extracting everything from your brain onto paper. It is also called a brain dump. Make sure you use a pen and paper for this process. There is something magical about using a pen and paper. Using a computer is nowhere near as effective. Believe me, I have tried. It just trumps your creativity. Using a pen and paper helps get your creative juices flowing.

Here, you list out everything you can think of about the book. The highlights, the points, the message, the stories, examples, pictures and other graphics, topics you want to cover, things you want to discuss etc. You start out with a theme or the title in the middle. Don't worry about getting the title right the first time. Sometimes you may find out that you have to change the title by the time you are done with the book and that's okay. I like to look at this as gathering all the bones for the skeleton. Leave no bone out.

Put the title in the middle and then just draw out lines from it to connect to bubbles or boxes where you write down all the ideas and things you want to be in the book. Don't worry about it being messy or ordered. Just dump everything. You do this for the book and also for each chapter. This ensures that everything you want to be in the book is there. You can cross out things later, it doesn't matter. The point here is to get everything out of your head until you have nothing left. It is not an outline so it doesn't have to be structured.

STEP 2: OUTLINE

After mind mapping your ideas onto paper, the next step is forming the structure of the book – the outline. You start by organising your mind map into sections. Group all the similar ideas together and assign a general theme for them. I like to look at this as constructing the skeleton of the book.

Organise these sections to create the order in the book. According to your mind map idea in each section, you should be able to tell which topics need to come before the other. These sections may not necessarily be whole chapters. Sections can contain enough material for several chapters.

Next you break up these sections into chapters that need

writing. Again, order the chapters accordingly to see which chapters need to come first. It doesn't have to be perfect. It just serves as a guide. Sometimes, after you finish writing the first draft, you may realise that you need to change the order of the chapters according to the information they provide. For guides such as this, that may not be a problem because the chapters iterate the step-by-step process for the guide.

STEP 3: WRITING

You are finally here, where you can begin writing your book. You have created your mind map, structured it into your outline and you pretty much know exactly what you are going to write about. Mind mapping and outlining your book makes it easy for your writing to flow and prevent writers' block. You can go from one sub-topic to another with ease, without ever pausing because you don't know what to write – unless you really don't know the topic you are writing about. This stage is where you flesh out the outline or the skeleton.

There is the temptation to want to make your first draft perfect, but by doing this, writers end up lengthening the process and they often don't finish the book. Remember, it is your first draft and it doesn't have to be perfect. The biggest milestone in book publishing is having a complete first draft. A complete, imperfect first draft is by far better than three perfectly done chapters of an incomplete book. The goal is to keep writing till you get to the end.

When you start writing, all you are doing is fleshing out your outline as I stated earlier. Start by writing about the first point, then follow the sequence all the way to the end. Do this for all the chapters including the introduction and conclusion and soon, you will have completed your first draft.

You want your book to flow, so it should have an introduction, the body (made up of the chapters) and the conclusion. Many people don't know what to write in the introduction and conclusion but there is an easy method of writing a flawless introduction, body and conclusion.

1. Tell them what you are going to tell them (Intro)
2. Tell them (Body)
3. Tell them what you told them (Conclusion).

What this simply means is that in the introduction, you create anticipation by telling them what to expect in the book. In the chapters, that is the body of the book, you tell them what you want to tell them. Finally, in the conclusion, you tell them what you told them in the chapters. Do this for each individual chapter too to create flow so your readers know what to expect in each chapter at the beginning and have a small summary of what was said in the chapter at the end.

One small secret to keep your readers interested in reading your book till the end is giving them a small piece of what they are going to read about in the next chapter at the end of your conclusion. This helps create anticipation and seamless flow. Introducing an introduction and conclusion for each chapter is a great way to bulk up your book.

WHAT IF I HATE WRITING?

Yes, I promised I was going to show you an easy way to get your book done even if you hate writing and I keep my promise. Follow the same process with the mind map – outline – write. You still have to pen down your mind map and outline. It is important that you do so. Some people use an app called Scrivena or a Trello board to do their outline but I'd rather you pen it down so you don't forget anything. Besides, when doing the outline, you may end up remembering more topics you want to add to your mind map and the outline.

For the writing part where most people have challenges, instead of writing, record yourself talking about each topic in your outline. Basically you are fleshing out your outline but instead of writing or typing, you are speaking it. It is super easy to do. You can get a lot done quicker if you record. Next, use Rev.com or TranscribeMe to transcribe your words. Rev.com charges about a dollar per minute. You can record on the app or record using your voice memo on your phone and manually send there. You can also source for a local transcriber in your area to transcribe the words for you. See? Simple!

WRITING YOUR BOOK IN RECORD TIME

It is easy for your writing to get lost in the day's activities. My job here is to make sure you write your book and publish it in the shortest time possible, but distractions won't make you do that. Here are the seven proven steps I used in writing my book in record time that you can also apply:

1. Always follow the three step process: mind map – outline – write.

2. Put yourself on the clock. Set blocks of time during the day for writing and don't stop till the time runs out.

3. Hurry up and write! You don't have to get to the end of this book before you begin writing. In the beginning, I advised you to take action steps as you read through. If you haven't been doing that, stop here, go back and start writing. You don't want to finish this book and then forget about it because you didn't start something.

4. Eliminate all distractions. Nothing trumps writing like distractions. Go to a quiet space when you want to write. Turn off your TV. Don't write when the kids are at home. Turn off your mobile phone and the Internet on your PC. No distractions!

5. Write first thing in the morning. If you have to go to work or get the kids ready for school, wake up one hour earlier and write. It is more effective to write in the morning when your day hasn't started to avoid it getting lost in the day's activities.

6. Be consistent. The more often you write, the better you will become and the faster you will finish your book. Writing for one hour everyday is better than writing for three hours a day, two times a week. Consistency is key. The more consistent you are, the harder it will be to not write.

7. Have an accountability partner. Having someone you report to, who holds you accountable, is one of the best things you can do for yourself, not just in writing, but in life generally. Tell everyone you're writing a book. Set a realistic deadline and tell everyone about it. That way, you know that there are a lot of people you have to prove something to. Then get someone you look up to, to hold you accountable. I can almost guarantee you that this is the single most important thing that has gotten a lot of writers to finish their book.

8. After you have written the main body of your book you can then add the dedication, foreword, copyright wording and legal disclaimers.

In the next chapter, I will show you how to edit your first draft, come up with a subtitle that pops and how to get your book cover done.

CHAPTER FOUR:

<u>EDITING, SUBTITLES AND BOOK COVER DESIGN</u>

Congratulations, you have finished your first draft! Now you can breathe a sigh of relief. You have done the most important part in book publishing. Remember that without a draft, there is nothing to edit, publish and sell. If you have gotten to this point, you are almost certainly going to be hitting the publish button pretty soon.

In this chapter, you will learn the simple process of editing your book, coming up with a cool subtitle that'll make buyers want to check out your book to see what it is about, and designing an eye-catching book cover design that stands out from your competition.

EDITING

When you have finished your first draft, the next step is editing. The first thing you should do is read your book out loud, preferably to someone's hearing. You can then make changes as you see fit, before you pass it on to an editor. When you read your book out loud, you can tell how the book is going to sound in the readers' head.

You can also get someone to read it out loud to you so that you can listen to the language of your book. Does it sound like you or a college professor (unless you are a college professor)? Does it flow? Is it making sense? Listen out for all these things. Sometimes you may want to rearrange the chapters so that there can be flow.

After reading and listening to your book, the next step is to send your book to a professional editor. I will advice you not to do the editing yourself. You wrote it yourself and you might miss some typos, misplaced paragraphs, double or missing words. A professional editor may also suggest synonyms that maybe better put into context the message you want to convey. Always keep in contact with your editor and keep track of the changes he/she makes so you are both on the same page (pun intended).

You can get your local editor to edit your work or you can find them on freelance sites like Elance, Freelancer and Fiverr. Fiverr is my favourite because you can literally get your work done for as low as $5 (Hence the name). You post your job on these sites and have people submit proposals. You can then vet and "interview" them to find the right fit for you. You want to make sure the person you select has a five star rating, has done several jobs, speaks the language of the book you are publishing, has positive reviews and samples of their work. They should also be able to meet your deadline and requirements.

BOOK SUBTITLE

Gone are the days when books had only one main title that could be as vague as they were misleading. Now, books have subtitles that clearly communicate what the book is about (and also because it is not practical to have these lengthy subtitles as the main title). A subtitle is like a mini sales pitch. It tells the reader what to expect and why they should buy your book, so you want to get it right. The clearer and more specific it is, the better it will be. So how do you pick a subtitle that converts browsers to buyers?

First, start with the benefits of the book. List them out on a sheet of paper. Then select the "attention grabber" benefits. These are the benefits you see that will instantly grab your attention. Next, speak to these benefits and make a BIG claim, but make sure it is something you can back up. No lies. Write this down. Write out ten examples and pick the best three.

When writing a subtitle, get out of your comfort zone. Don't be modest in your subtitles. People want to see results and you have to show them that your book can provide them the results they want. Be bold and more specific. Speak directly to the reader. Don't worry about starting with the keywords for your niche. Start with the benefits. A book full of keywords and an "empty" subtitle will sell way less than a subtitle without keywords.

DESIGNING YOUR STUNNING BOOK COVER

Unless you are a pretty darn good graphics designer, I will suggest you get your book cover done by a professional. You can get good book covers on Fiverr from as low as $5. That is nothing compared to shooting yourself in the foot with an amazing book that has an ugly or poorly done Book cover.

When it comes to a e-Book publishing, the phrase "don't judge a book by its cover" does not apply. There are literally millions of books on Amazon so you want yours to jump out at readers. Remember Amazon puts thumbnail versions of your book cover on display so it has to be catchy enough to make a reader stop scrolling and click on it. Follow the same process of sourcing for editors on freelance sites to source for e-book cover designers. They will usually send you mock ups for you to choose from. Always request for different formats like Amazon kindle, 3-D format and Front and back cover designs. You will be using these different formats in your publishing and marketing.

Next up, you want to get feedback for your book covers from family and friends, social media audience and your mailing list. This is a great way to pre-advertise your book and let people know you are putting out a book. People will be excited to be part of your book publishing process when you ask their opinion on stuff like the book cover design. It builds anticipation and eases the advertising, launch and marketing process. You can take a few of the ones you like and a terrible one and ask them to choose.

QUICK TIP: Once your book makes it to the bestsellers list, you can go back and edit your book cover on Amazon, even though your book has been published, and add the "Amazon Bestseller" to the cover if you choose. Everyone loves the orange banner.

HOW DO I KNOW A GOOD BOOK COVER WHEN I SEE ONE?

Do your research. Look for book covers in your niche and see what sells, not just what looks good. Remember these points to guide you when searching for a good book cover:

- People should be able to read the title on the book cover without having to squint or zoom in. Think Amazon thumbnail.
- It should not look bland and dull.
- The title should not be vague. It must be clear.
- The cover should jump out at you. It should make you pause when scrolling.
- It should clearly display the message with graphics, colour and the subtitle.
- If you have a catch (like a freebie inside), put it on the book cover and it should be clear.

A WORD OF CAUTION

It is easy to get stuck in the final process or finishing your book. You want the editing and book cover to be perfect. There is the fear that your book might not be good enough – that you are not good enough. Don't. Remember, DONE IS BETTER THAN PERFECT. Don't get stuck in the editing process. It is an e-Book, you can always change things after you have published. Set a launch date and tell people about it. Just hit publish.

CHAPTER FIVE:

PUBLISHING ON AMAZON

Publishing your book on Amazon Kindle is very easy. The challenge most people have is where to get started and in what format the book should be. By now you should have finished with the editing and you should have selected your attention grabbing book cover. It is important to note that you should have a copy of just the book cover on your PC because you will need to upload it separately.

Here is the step-by-step process to publish your book on Amazon Kindle:

1. Go to kdp.amazon.com and open an Amazon kindle authors account. KDP stands for Kindle Direct Publishing. If you have an Amazon account already, you can use that to sign into your Kindle Account. You will need to fill in some details such as your name and address, contacts, tax information (if you are using amazon.com and you have a USA bank account), Bank account details and a few other things. If you are going to be receiving your royalties by check (if you are outside the US), you want to make sure you fill in your correct home address.

2. Decide on KDP or KDP Select. With KDP Select, you cannot sell your digital book on other online stores for the duration of 90 days, after which your KDP select option can be cancelled or renewed. If you are planning

on launching on multiple platforms like iBooks and Nook, or your website, you don't want to select this option. The upside to KDP select is that you can run free promotions or discounted promotions for up to 5 days and then the price automatically reverts back to the original price you set.

3. Sign into Amazon Kindle and go to your bookshelf. If you have never published a book before, your shelf will be empty. Go to "create a new title" to add your book to your bookshelf and click on "+Kindle eBook". Follow the easy prompts to fill in the information for your book such as author name(s), book description, categories, countries to publish in (I say go global), Price and other information.

4. You will see the prompt to upload your book cover. Read the guidelines to ensure your book cover meets the quality guidelines. Your graphic artist should know these guidelines so he/she will create a book cover that meets the quality requirements. You don't upload 3-D covers or front and back covers to Amazon Kindle eBook publishing. Your book cover should be 1563px by 2500px image. Amazon recommends 1.6 height:width ratio.

5. Next, you will need to upload your manuscript. I usually recommend that your manuscript is converted to .pdf or .mobi before uploading. Amazon uses the .mobi format, but if you cannot convert your manuscript to .mobi before uploading, that's okay. Amazon has a file

converter that you can download in the upload section that will automatically convert your file to the required format. A scan of your manuscript will usually be done to make sure it meets their content and quality guidelines but Amazon isn't really strict on content. Remember you can edit the cover and any part of your book at any time.

6. You can preview your book to see how it will look when a reader checks it out. It is important to preview your book before publishing to check for any errors that might have occurred with your upload.

7. Set your pricing. eBooks that are priced between $0.99 - 10.99 get 70% royalty as Amazon takes 30% of any sales, while eBooks above $10.99 get 35% royalty as Amazon takes 65% of any sales. So the higher the price of your book, the smaller the royalty you earn. It is recommended that you don't go beyond $4.99 for eBooks. The sweet spot for eBook profits is $2.99 - 4.99. Anything higher does not usually sell well. If you are unsure about what price to set, Amazon can suggest a price based on the size, title and category of your book.

8. When choosing the category for your book, refer to the research you did while coming up with the idea for your book as we discussed in Chapter 2. Stick to that category. Also look out for the keywords that stood out and use those ones. You can put up to 7 keywords for your book. Use those same keywords in the description of your book to boost your visibility on Amazon kindle. This is why it

is very important to research your book's category. The wrong category can kill your chances of making sales.

9. Go over the required boxes to check that you did not miss anything. When choosing where to publish, choose to publish worldwide. That way, your book gets more visibility and you get more profits. My book has sold in every continent and in over 13 countries to date. It is really exciting to see my book reaching people in places I may never even go to.

10. HIT PUBLISH. Of all the buttons you have clicked so far, this is the most satisfying one to click, I assure you. It is also one of the hardest ones to click. Of course you know that you can always take down your books if you choose or edit the content of your books, but still, it can be nerve-wracking for some people. This is the moment you have been waiting for and it's finally here. When you hit that publish button, you officially become an author. It is one of the most amazing feelings ever! It usually takes 24 - 48 hours for the book to go live, so you want to publish at least 48 hours before you launch.

Launching your book is the next step after you hit publish. In the next chapter, I will show you a super-easy and inexpensive way to launch your book and be on your way to an Amazon bestseller. Keep reading.

CHAPTER SIX:

<u>THE LAUNCH</u>

Launching a book is where most people get really confused. Especially if it's an e-Book. The truth is, launching an e-Book is way easier and cheaper than launching a book in print. In fact, when launching an e-Book, you don't even need to have a physical event. You can have an epic launch online and make massive publicity and sales. It is also important to know that launching your e-Book doesn't begin after you hit publish.

The launch begins from the moment you begin to tell people that you are writing your book. In fact it actually begins after you have found your book idea. The advantage of this is that it builds awareness and curiosity about your book, and the more people know about your book, the better for you. After you hit publish, you can then do a major noisemaking launch. This launch is what I like to call the "official launch day".

So how do you launch your book?

1. Create a buzz around your book. Let people know you are writing a book. Talk about what the book is about to your family, friends, social media audience and email list if you have one already. In the weeks before you launch, you want to talk about your book as as much as possible because the more people hear it, the more likely they are to remember you and your book. This also creates curiosity as more people will look forward to buying your

book just to see what the fuss is all about. Hey, the goal is to get them to buy, right? You create buzz by talking to people about it, writing social media posts, blog posts and email newsletters.

2. Get your audience to be part of the process. Talk about your ideas for the book. Share your challenges with them. Get them to help pick out your book cover. Update them on your different milestones as you are achieving them. The more your audience gets involved, the less it feels like your book and the more it feels like their book. When your book is finally published, they will be more than happy to see the fruit of "their" labour.

3. Pick a launch date and let your audience countdown with you. This builds excitement in your audience because they have been part of the process and will want to see the success of your book. Create a countdown on your social media pages and email newsletters. If you have a Facebook page or community (which, by the way you really should have), create an event for your launch date and post reminders as the day draws near. It is okay to pick a launch date before your book is finished. This helps you to actually finish the book on time and makes you accountable to all those people who know about your launch date. It is extra motivation for you.

4. My super-secret tip to multiple book downloads on your launch comes next. This is something I accidentally did when launching my first book, that proved to be one of

the biggest factors for the book's success. I had no email list, no blog and no Facebook page or community at the time. So even if you have none of these, you can still have a huge launch and crazy downloads on your launch day.

What I did was to join large Facebook communities that had my target audience – people who I knew wouldn't mind having a free copy of my book. That's another thing – when launching your book on Amazon, it is smart to give away your book for free for a couple of days if you are using Kindle Select. This helps you build momentum and catapults you to the Amazon bestsellers list. Because of the spike in downloads, Amazon will suggest your book to readers in your niche for free just like Facebook does with pages and groups.

After joining these Facebook communities in the weeks before my launch, I created a buzz there just like I did on my Facebook profile and my other social media platforms but I kept it non-spammy. You don't want to be chased out of a Facebook community for spamming people with your book talk. Here's what I did: I had them answer questions about topics in my book, created a poll for opinions on the best subtitle for my book, and had them pick out my book cover. People in communities are generally nice and supportive and will readily download your book when it launches. If you haven't joined a Facebook community yet, join one now.

5. Free publicity. While creating buzz on your social media platforms, email lists and niched Facebook communities is

awesome, you need to be armed with as many weapons as possible. You know, there is no such thing as too much publicity when it comes to launching your book. If you have friends with large social media following or large email lists, you can reach out to them to help you publicise your book right before your launch. A lot of people don't think of this. There is no harm in asking.

If you don't have friends like this, look for influencers in your niche, connect with them and get to work. You don't go asking strangers to help you publicise your book for free. You have to give them something in return. You can offer to promote their paid programs to your audience if they can help promote your book either via social media posts, email newsletters with a link to download your book or a podcast interview. Give them a good reason why they should promote your book. By the time you are armed to the teeth with all these tools, you can't escape the Amazon bestsellers list.

6. The Amazon marketing system. This is where KDP Select is useful. If you plan on publishing your book on only Amazon, I suggest you use KDP Select when publishing your book. When uploading your book, you can sign up for the KDP Select and set your book at a price between $2.99 and $9.99, so when you activate KDP Selects's free promo which can run for up to 5 days, Amazon's marketing will go something like this: "You save $2.99" (or whatever price you set), and then strike through the original price. The more people have to save in buying your book, the more they will be willing to buy it. People always love a good bargain. Just

remember, you are not allowed to publish on any other platform but Amazon if you opt in for the KDP Select. Amazon gains exclusive rights and will penalise you if they find out you have violated their terms.

You may be asking why you have to give away lots of your book for free when you clearly want to make money. The reason is this: even though you don't make any money during the free promo period, your success this time by the number of downloads your book will have, will lead you to making more money when your book changes from free to paid. This is because you will get support from Amazon when they start to feature your book on other people's book pages and suggest your book to their readers in newsletters.

If you are going to publish your book on your website and other platforms, you can set your book price to $0.99 on Amazon. It's almost as good as free and people usually have no problem paying $0.99 even if they are not sure of the quality of the book.

7. The launch. Most successful authors who have published on Amazon kindle agree that Tuesday is the best day of the week to do a launch. Traditionally, book launches and even music album releases are on Tuesday because the Monday craze has died down and the call of the weekend hasn't started to distract people yet.

This however becomes problematic when you want to run a 5-day promo because two of those days (Friday and Saturday) are dead days. People don't usually want to buy books on the weekend. The solution is to either launch on Tuesday with a 3-day promo or launch on Sunday with a 5-day promo. Launching on Sunday can also give you a head start to your competition by climbing the charts.

Please note that when launching, announce the number of days the promo will run for (I usually suggest you say 2-3 days even if you are doing a 5-day promo as it creates a sense of urgency when the time is short).

Remember to send out posts, messages, email newsletters and even live broadcasts on the day of your launch to remind people about it. A lot of people just let the launch day come and put up one social media post and hope for the best. It doesn't work that way. Your launch day is when you and your friends make all the noise you possibly can and get everyone to download your book. Put up posts in the morning, noon and evening, and before you go to bed, to allow for the time zone differences. This ensures everyone who comes online has the chance to see your launch posts. Also remind people to leave reviews. The more the positive reviews, the better for you.

8. Social media ads. If you have a couple of dollars to spare, a very well targeted social media ad on Facebook, Instagram and Twitter will go a long way in boosting your downloads, especially when people see that it is free. A very good $20 ad that runs for 2 to 3 days can reach hundreds of thousands of your potential readers. If you only get 1% of those people to download your book, that's an Amazon bestseller knocking

on your door.

9. Gradually work up your price. After the launch, the hundreds or thousands of downloads and the Amazon bestseller status, it is time to start making the money. Gradually bump up the price a dollar at a time. Start at $0.99 and then $1.99 a week later or so. Remember to stay within the sweet spot for eBooks. Any higher than this and people may not buy.

Launching your book is an exciting phase. You are officially presenting the gift that is your book to the world. You should be proud of yourself and your accomplishments. Some people might get cold feet when launching because they are afraid of negative reviews, or they feel that they and their book are not good enough. That's not true. You have written a book, which is more than millions of wannabes have ever done. Be proud of yourself. You are special.

CHAPTER SEVEN:

MARKETING YOUR BOOK EFFECTIVELY

Marketing your book does not end after your launch. It is a continuous process, especially if you want to make money off it. Many people launch and then stop promoting their book, hoping people will continue to buy. It doesn't always work like that. If you stop marketing your book and promoting it, all you will get are trickles in sales. You want to maximise every avenue and opportunity you have to make sales.

There are several ways to market your book after launch to ensure continued profits besides repurposing your book's contents which I will discuss in the next chapter. Your book is not meant to sit on your virtual bookshelf and gather "dust". At every opportunity you get, promote your book. As a self published author, you are practically responsible for the success of your book from A to Z, and that includes the continuous promotion and marketing.

Traditional writers just write and let the publishers take care of everything else, but unless you have the funds to hire a marketer, you do it yourself. When you begin to treat your e-Book as a business, it will yield serious profits for you. You need to get your hands and feet dirty in the self promoting and book promoting business. I know you don't like it, but hey, it has to be done if you want your book to stay profitable.

For most people, marketing isn't a natural thing, but

fortunately, book marketing isn't so hard, especially when it's an eBook. It won't be hard to learn the basic skills in marketing. So here are some easy ways you can market your book:

1. Make sure in the book description box, you write a killer sales page that compels people to want to buy. A book description is not about the features of the book, instead it is about how the book benefits the reader. You want them to hit the "buy now" button before they even get to the end of the description.

2. Most self published authors forget one very vital part of marketing on Amazon - the Author Central page. After creating your kindle account, go to the navigation box on the right to create your Amazon author page and add your book there or go to authorcentral.amazon.com . Here, readers can find your author profile and get to know you. As you write more books, they can see a list of all your books there.

3. Ask for reviews from your readers. Reviews are like testimonials that you can publish to your audience to convince doubting minds that your book is really good. Don't be ashamed to ask for those reviews, Baby! The more the reviews (especially positive ones), the more people are compelled to buy.

4. Keep track of your metrics. I suggest you obsess about your stats at least for the first two weeks. Check your reviews daily, check your rankings as often as hourly if

you can (ranks and bestseller lists are updated hourly), check your sales daily and keep track of the number of countries your book has been sold in. Most importantly, keep an eye out for the bestsellers list. You don't want to miss when your book makes it to the bestsellers list. That was a mistake I made with my first book. I checked all stats but that one and missed when it made the top of the bestsellers list. Take screenshots for social proof like the one in the intro here. Remember, you want to be able to show your fans that it did happen.

The more successful your book does, the more people are compelled to buy. Post your successes on your social media platforms, blogs and email newsletters and don't forget to appreciate your audience for buying. Others may feel "guilty" for not buying and will want to rid their guilt by going to buy, even after the free promo is over, just to be part of the success and appreciation going round. This is called "psychological selling".

5. Promote your book on other platforms. Write and submit guest posts that support your book. Some bloggers can allow you to post a back link to your book. Share important quotes from your book on social media. Have a link to download your book in your social media bio. Continue to link to your book in blog posts, social media updates and email signatures. Do podcast interviews, and if you can, get on TV and radio shows to promote your book.

6. Plan cross-promotions with a friend or an influencer who also has their book out. You promote each others books or create incentives like competitions for your audience to win free copies. This is a great way to reward your loyal audience.

7. Do a free webinar and upsell your book. A free webinar on one topic or chapter in your book is a great way to really target a potential audience who will be interested in buying your book. You can run a Facebook targeted ad and have people sign up for your free webinar. Because your webinar topic is from your book, there is a greater chance of them actually buying your book when you upsell. I will suggest offering your book at a more discounted price than the original price at the upsell. This is another reason for people to want to buy. For example, you can say that your book can be gotten at $1.99 instead of $4.99 for a limited time.

8. Use Amazon's Marketing Service to promote your book to Amazon's reader community. This works like Facebook ads but Amazon uses the keywords of your book to target their readers when they search for books relating to the keywords you have used. This is a more effective way to get more targeted sales for your book as the target audience are already looking to buy what you are selling. They will also suggest your book to readers in their mailing list.

9. You can also make a series of teaching videos around

your book topic on YouTube or your website and then upsell your book. You don't want to offer a limited discount Price on these type of videos because they are going to be there forever where anyone can find them at any time until you take it down.

10. Publish your book on other platforms like Nook, iBooks, Smashwords, Nerveflo (Nigeria), Okadabooks (Nigeria) and other online bookstores if you are not on Amazon KDP Select or after the first 90 days of being on KDP Select and you do not wish to continue. You can also sell your book on your website using Woo Commerce or Shopify. If you are on Kindle Select and you want to feature your book on your website, you can put the book cover on your shop and then link it to your book on Amazon. The more platforms you have your book on, the wider your chances are of reaching even more readers. Also remember to update your book on Goodreads and similar sites so that reviewers can see, read and review your book.

11. Convert your book into print using Amazon Create Space and into an audiobook using Amazon's Audible (ACX). By converting your book into different formats, you are able to reach an audience that your eBook alone will not reach. Some people still prefer print copy and others would rather listen to a book than read it. The more readers you can reach, the more books you can sell. Besides, print and audiobooks are priced higher than eBooks.

HOW TO USE CREATESPACE TO CONVERT YOUR EBOOK INTO PRINT

Createspace is Amazon's miracle for self published authors. With Createspace, you can easily turn your eBook to print practically for free and publish it in the prints section. Amazon just takes a tiny bit of the price in printing and calculates shipping separately. How this works is that Amazon prints high quality versions of your book on demand when a book order is made. You don't have to pay thousands of dollars for printing or even worry about shipping.

Print books are generally priced higher so your eBook can cost 3 times as much in print and you didn't even have to do any work and you still get to make lots of profit. The same thing goes for audiobooks in Audible. The best part is, after the book has been published in print, you can then order several copies and have them shipped to you so you can stock them in your local bookshops and give as gifts to friends and family or even keep one for yourself. Imagine holding your own book in your hands. As you can see, the possibilities for profit from just one eBook are almost endless. There is still so much you can do with this one book that I will show you in the next chapter, but for now, here's a few things you should know before converting your book into print:

- Converting your book into print using Createspace is as easy as publishing your eBook on Amazon, if not easier. You can literally do it in minutes.

- Your book must be up to 24 pages long for Amazon to make it into print. Any less and Amazon will suggest you revise your book before converting it.

- An ISBN number is required to publish and distribute your book. You can opt to ask Amazon to automatically generate one for you for free.

Now that we've cleared that up, here is the step by step process to converting your eBook to print using Createspace:

1. Set up a free publishing account on Createspace. This can be done when you go to your book shelf and click on "+Print book" and start a project for your book. As with your eBook, follow the step by step prompts that are clearly shown.

2. Write an effective book description or copy the one from your eBook description.

3. Opt for Createspace to assign your book a free ISBN.

4. Upload the interior content of the book (i.e the eBook file). Createspace will usually ask if you want it in black and white or coloured. If you have graphics in your book, opt for the coloured to make them appear better. If not, opt for black and white. Black and white costs less. Note that this does not affect the book cover, just the interior of the book.

5. Select the size of your book. The default size is 6 by 9

but most books are usually done in 5.25 by 8. It is better to go for the popular choice.

6. Upload your eBook cover. this time, you are uploading the front and back cover, not the same one you used for your eBook. This is why you must ask your eBook designer to create the different formats for your book cover. Upload your book cover to the cover creator to automatically format the cover to the right format based on your book's size and the page content. If you do not have a cover with front and back, you can use Creatspace's book cover templates to create one using your eBook cover's photos, logos and text. The "Palm" template usually works best.

7. Preview your book to see what it will look like and update if necessary. You can download the pdf proof and study it carefully first to make any necessary changes before you finally publish, then buy a copy.

8. Choose your pricing and distribution. Once again, I suggest to choose worldwide for your distribution. Print books cost more than the e-Book version. If people are viewing the print version of your book, Amazon usually suggests that the e-Book version is available. Once they see that the e-Book costs way less, they usually opt for that instead, leading to more sales for your e-Book. Publishers suggest pricing your print book at 3X the price of your e-Book. I suggest you price between $7.99 and $14.99. That's the sweet spot.

That's a priceless secret that self published authors use to print their books, rather than depend on publishers and printers and spend thousands of dollars. In the next chapter, I will be showing you how to turn your one book into multiple streams of income. You don't have to keep writing more and more books to make a steady income and I will show you how.

CHAPTER EIGHT:

REPURPOSING YOUR EBOOK CONTENT FOR MORE PROFIT

Profiting from your book doesn't have to end in book sales alone. There are so many ways you can create multiple streams of income from your book by repurposing the content in several ways that can be monetised both directly and indirectly. Writing a book can help you launch a new career selling what you know by being an information entrepreneur or infopreneur.

Writing The Productivity Checklist helped establish me as an authority on productivity for people who work from home and opened the doors to my career as a Mindset Coach. The various ways I have been able to make money and gain exposure teaching what I know couldn't have happened without that tiny book.

I have benefited from writing a book in terms of value addition, community building, podcasts, interviews, magazine features and YouTube shows, guest posts on blogs, speaking engagements, authority status, exposure and intentional networking. People who I would have otherwise not been able to network with, have now become friends. I have amazing mentors and colleagues in the thought leadership industry both in Nigeria and abroad and the exposure has been tremendous. There is hardly any local event I attend where someone doesn't recognise me. All this because of a 19-page book.

Enough about me. You can also achieve all these and more by learning how to milk every last drop of opportunity that writing your book provides. Here are a few ways that you can do that:

1. BLOG CONTENT: You can start a blog and create blog content from your book by choosing a topic from your book and expanding on it or summarising it, depending on the size of the content in the topic you have written in your book. It is also a great way to start blogging if you don't have a blog yet. You can then create a reader audience from your blog and direct people to your book for more information about the topic.

2. SOCIAL MEDIA CONTENT: Many people struggle with staying consistent on social media. You can repurpose you content from your book into social media posts, turn quotes into beautiful graphics or create polls on a particular topic in your book. You can't run out of content for social media posts, especially if you engage your audience and answer their questions on your posts. It is also a great way to build community on social media, especially on Facebook.

3. WEBINARS: Free and paid webinars are also a good way to generate leads for your email list and upsell your book, online courses or coaching programs. Webinars are fast becoming one of the most effective lead generation tools for sales funnels and you can cash in on that by creating

webinars around your book topic.

4. LIVE MASTERCLASS: For people who like meeting with other people and hosting seminars, this is a great source of income, especially if you have begun to build influence. By engaging with your audience, you will be able to tell when they want a live meet up and most times, they will be willing to pay to have a live masterclass or seminar where you can expound on one or more topics in your book.

5. ONLINE COURSES: Online courses are my favourite. I have been able to generate six-figure income from online courses alone. I start by offering a freebie, then doing a webinar or a Facebook live broadcast to my online community where I teach a particular topic and then upsell my online course at the end of the webinar. The conversion rates are very encouraging. I have gone on to teach online courses on subjects not relating to productivity, but writing that book gave me the opportunity to leverage on my authority and credibility to explore my other knowledge areas. The great thing about online courses is that you don't even have to show your face if you don't want to. You can create voice-over slides and deliver them to your students via email. You can also upload them to your website and sell them again and again, or upload them to learning management systems like Teachable, Thinkific, Skillshare, Udemy, Coursera Kajabi and the like.

6. COACHING: Here's a fun fact: I wrote a book on productivity and it launched my career as a Mindset Coach. How did I do it, you ask? I leveraged on the exposure and credibility that being an author provided me, and began creating content relating to mindset and performance. It wasn't long till my audience began to refer to me as a Mindset Coach. I was intentional in my content creation and delivery and the audience caught on. I had to get certified as a coach though, to back up the title. Today however, I can say that in the thought leadership niche here in Nigeria, if you are looking for a mindset coach, my name comes to mind. Being a mindset coach has accorded me opportunities to speak at events, facilitate panel discussions, be interviewed on podcasts, and has put me in the elite circle of coaches. It all traces back to that one book I wrote.

7. PODCASTS: Podcasts are another great way to repurpose your book's content. You can record audio versions of the different topics in your book and upload them to Podcast and Sound Cloud. With consistency and persistence, you can build a large audience and begin to have sponsors for your podcasts. Once your podcast begins to get noticed, you'll have no trouble connecting to "Rock stars" in your industry and interviewing them on your podcast and vice versa, thereby getting a share of their audience.

8. WORKBOOKS, JOURNALS AND MERCHANDISE: If your eBook is a guide or a "how-to", just like this one, you can create workbooks on your book's content on the action plans and sell it separately, either as a digital copy or print or both. The same goes for journals. As your book and yourself become a brand, you can start creating merchandise like snap backs, shirts, mugs, branded journals and the like, just like Grant Cardone did with his 10X book. This is another great way to create multiple streams of income, especially if you can get celebrities to wear or use your merchandise.

The list of ways you can repurpose your book's content or leverage on your book to create multiple streams of income is endless. You don't have to do all of them; just start with the one you are most comfortable with and then grow from there. As you grow, you may just discover your own unique way of generating income, launching your new career or boosting your already existing career.

Today, I not only write books, coach and teach online courses, I also help people through this process from writing their books to creating a profitable online business from home that can enable them leave their boring jobs, do what they love and have fun while making lots of money doing it. For me, this is the real profit. What will your own story be? Start now to write it. Literarily.

CONCLUSION

The process of writing your book, publishing it and profiting from it is really an easy process. The only thing standing between you and your goal of becoming a published author is your excuse, and I believe that whatever excuse you have has been dealt with in this book.

I have carefully iterated all the steps to help you go from no idea whatsoever, to being an accomplished author and then some. If you are thinking of profiting from your eBook, I have also covered that in the marketing and profit-making chapters of this book.

The steps in this books are so simple, anyone can literally follow them and become a rockstar author in six weeks or less. It took me twelve days to go from idea to a finished first draft for this book. If you are willing to follow these steps, nothing can stop you from achieving your dream; and not just publishing, but also profiting immensely from it. I hope you write your book and share it with the rest of the world. You deserve to live your dreams. I wish you all the best!

ABOUT THE AUTHOR

Edirin Edewor is an award-winning Entrepreneur, an Author, Mindset Coach and a Personal Development Speaker. She has started a movement in Nigeria where she educates people on the importance of having the right mindset for peak performance and success, a subject that until now has been quite vague to many business people.

She helps business owners get clarity in their core message and helps them start and grow their businesses by employing simple strategies for success, drawing from her years of experience in business. She Coaches a community of more than a thousand entrepreneurs twice a week via live broadcast and has also helped other thought leaders and entrepreneurs write and publish their books in record time.

When she isn't working, Edirin volunteers at several non-profit organisations geared towards child education and women empowerment. She is also a regular anonymous donor at several local and international organisations to help fund research for diseases. Edirin lives in Lagos, Nigeria and loves writing, food, fitness and travel.

CONNECT WITH ME

Thank you for buying and reading this book. Please remember to leave reviews and connect with me on my blog and social media platforms:

www.edirinedewor.com

Mail: edirin@edirinedewor.com

Join my Facebook community to connect with other authors, aspiring authors and freelancers where you can promote your book and receive more book publishing and profit tips at facebook.com/groups/ebookprofitsmastery

Instagram: @edirinedewor

Twitter: @edirinedewor

www.ingramcontent.com/pod-product-compliance
Lightning Source LLC
Chambersburg PA
CBHW020708180526
45163CB00008B/2998